Revels of Fancy

Revels of Fancy.

BY

WILLIAM JOHNSON VANDYNE.

Writer or feaster, there 's not a guest
Who will not find some piece ill-drest.
— Sir Howard.

The Black Heritage Library Collection

BOOKS FOR LIBRARIES PRESS
FREEPORT, NEW YORK
1971

First Published 1891
Reprinted 1971

Reprinted from a copy in the
Fisk University Library Negro Collection

INTERNATIONAL STANDARD BOOK NUMBER:
0-8369-8933-3

LIBRARY OF CONGRESS CATALOG CARD NUMBER:
71-179297

PRINTED IN THE UNITED STATES OF AMERICA
BY
NEW WORLD BOOK MANUFACTURING CO., INC.
HALLANDALE, FLORIDA 33009

Dear Mr. Johnson Vandyne:

You have asked me to look over your poems from time to time. I have done so with pleasure, accepting many, and have felt that they possessed merit, and that the development of your poetic gift should be in every way encouraged, as there needs some pen to voice thoughts and sentiments of your own people and your verse catches the sentiment of the times.

I advised you to study the best models of verse, to seek to do better and more perfect work, for "every man is a debtor to his profession." How well you have tried to follow this advice, your beautiful and sympathetic poem on Touissant L'Ouverture shows. I have read that poem with especial delight as a piece of literary work, and have been touched that you seem to have caught the spirit of the Liberator and Martyr. The work of your methods and thoughts as shown in this poem, make you worthy of every encouragement, and I am glad that you are about to publish your poems in book form, and I wish, as every one who loves progress will, that the book may receive merited recognition and be most successful.

If you can produce such pieces to-day, you can do much perfect work in the future, and there are many leaders like Touissant whose spirit you may well interpret.

Cordially yours,

HEZEKIAH BUTTERWORTH,

Assistant Editor of Youth's Companion.

November, 23d, 1891.

PRELUDE.

Who spreads the banquet
  Has a royal heart,
And friends on friends
  His praises love to tell.
Then if those things
  Such regal joys impart
Why not the luxuries
  Of lore as well?
I 've whiled away
  Some scanty hours of ease
In picturing man
  So frail and hard to please, —
Now, if perchance
  Some feel too much abused,
I cannot kneel,
  But beg to be excused.

WM. JOHNSON VANDYNE.

REVELS OF FANCY.

KNOWLEDGE.

Knowledge, the lamp of genius, full and free,
    Thou art a guardian angel clothed in light;
How dumb, we mortals, were it not for thee
    To guide us through the centuries of night !
Beneath the power of thy magic wand
    The dark delusions of the past have fled,
And shrines of ignorance no longer stand,
    Around which blinded nations fought and bled.

'Tis at thy shrine the future statesman dwells,
    And learns the secret of an empire's weal,
And Science, to her son and daughter, tells
    The mysteries deep that some can only feel;
'Tis thine to solve the puzzle of the skies,
    And cast a light upon the dark eclipse ;
To pluck the fury from Dissension's eyes,
    And sip the honey from Apollo's lips.

Thy children rise, no matter how obscure,
    And often mount the pinnacle of fame;
And all who enter at thy golden door
    Are made more alien to the sting of shame;

9

Thine is the power of eloquence sublime;
   Thine is the wonderous wisdom of the age;
Thine is the logic of the poet's rhyme,
   And triumphs of discoverer and sage.

Then come, O glorious Knowledge, evermore,
   And smile upon all nations on the earth!
Long may thy temples gleam on every shore
   As emblems of an empire's weal and worth:
Long may the toilers, who to fame aspire,
   Trust to the power of thy eagle wings,
And mount the lofty summit higher and higher
   To gain the golden fruit that labor brings.

———

GEMS OF THOUGHT.

The glittering gold comes from the mine
   By toiling, constant toiling;
The bee receives his saccharine
   By spoiling, constant spoiling;
And gems of thought, cannot be brought
   From fancy's fountain chiming,
But must be wooed by careful brood
   And rhyming, constant rhyming.

THE OLD VETERAN.

" Say, father, who is that poor old man
    That I met on the green to-day?
His wrinkled brow had many a scar,
    And his hair was long and gray ;
And he told us a tale of battles wild,
    Of the pride of the gray and blue :
I guess he was one of those true and tried
    That charged at Waterloo !"

" Oh ! no, my son, he was better armed,
    And fought for a nobler cause
Than the veterans I have told you of
    In Napoleon's endless wars :
He fought that the light of a land might live—
    That a nation might be free ;
And he charged with the dash
    Of that grand old guard in all their chivalry."

Then the father told him of Gettysburgh,
    And of Sherman's march to the sea;
Of Sheridan's ride on his coal-black steed,
    Of the songs of the brave and free ;
And he quothed with eyes of heroic fire :
    " Long wave the flag of the blue ;
I will stand it by, on land or sea
    Like the guard of Waterloo! "

THE CROSSING OF THE DELAWARE.

Upon that bleak December night,
    When warriors bold and maidens fair
Met 'neath the glowing astral's light,
    In old halls on the Delaware,

The Hessians' hearts were light and gay
    As if they revelled on the Rhine,
And chased the golden hours away
    With dance and wit and flow of wine.

And merry all, and gay and bright,
    The warrior brave, the maiden fair,
When broke a sound upon the night,
    Mysterious, from the Delaware.

From halls of light, and music gay,
    They form upon the frozen field,
And meet, on that immortal day,
    The spirit that can never yield.

Oh! band of patriots, few and bold,
    That mantled crossed to Jersey's shore;
The night was dark, the night was cold,
    But freedom lay thy barks before.

No more, when halls are gay and light,
    These warriors brave and maidens fair
Will dance, as on that fateful night
    When freedom crossed the Delaware.

'Tis well the tyrant's power was broke,
    The deed inspired the future sage;
And Freedom's voice much louder spoke
    To break the chain a future age.

THE WRECK OF THE CITY OF COLUMBUS.

Calm was the night,
The moon shone bright
Upon the silent sea;
And the vessel rode
With its precious load
As smooth as smooth could be.

The minstrel sang,
The gay laugh rang,
The cornet sweetly played;
And the heart beat time
To the mellow rhyme
Of the waltz and promenade.

Long did they sail,
There came no gale,
The waves beat soft and dull;"
When a sudden shock,
As of a rock,
Came o'er that mighty hull.

" To the leeward side,"
The captain cried,
" And all is safe and well;
But the eyes so mild
Took an aspect wild,
And fear no tongue could quell.

All, all in vain.
Like the surging main,
Each one rushed here and there;

"A boat! a boat!
Or' a log to float!"
Was the wild cry everywhere.

The shout and scream
Woke the quiet dream
Of the sleepers down below;
And their cheeks turned white,
At an awful sight,
And they hurried to and fro.

"She is sinking fast!
We must climb the mast!"
Cried out a sailor brave;
But they saw Death's frown;
And the ship went down
With all, to watery grave.

Then the mighty sea
Seemed to laugh with glee,
As he smoothed his surface o'er;
And the moon shone bright
On the calm, clear night;
But the ship was seen no more.

───────

PERSEVERANCE.

Most any art, if followed fast,
Its lover will reward at last;
Then faint not on the rugged way
For night is but the friend of day.

THE BELL AMONG THE HILLS.

Oh, hear the bell among the hills,
The balmy air with music fills,
For sweetly in the purple dell,
At twilight rings the village bell;
And when it rings at close of day,
I dream of hours long passed away.
My heart with joy and ardor fills
To hear the bell among the hills.

For that sweet bell among the hills.
That all the air with music fills,
I heard in long departed years,
When joy was unalloyed with fears;
And though they long have passed away
I see their pictures bright to-day;
And soothing power my spirit fills,
To hear the bell among the hills.

Ring on! sweet bells among the hills;
When all the West with splendor fills,
And like a fairy river's flow
Bring back sweet dreams of long ago ;
For now I tread a barren soil,
And climb the rugged heights of toil;
But still my heart with pleasure thrills,
To hear the bell among the hills.

SHE WAS A BEAUTY.

She was a beauty, yet her face
  Was not so fair to see;
Her form had not the classic grace
  Of perfect symmetry,
Her eyes were not like violets blue,
  That grace the garden close,
Her cheeks had not the radient hue
  That decks the summer rose.

She was a beauty, for her mind
  Was free from foolish pride,
She never spoke a word unkind
  But scatterred blessings wide;
Her smile stole in the heart of care,
  A sunbeam's cheering ray;
She was a beauty, grand and fair,
  Whose power grew day by day.

THE FATE OF ALL.

The king and queen, from their royal state,
  Soon must descend to die;
And even the greatest of the great
  In the sombre tomb must lie;
The throne of gems, and the crown of gold,
  The robe of purple hue
Is by the hand of time controlled,
  Like the gems of sparkling dew.

SUNSET.

Sunset soft and slowly fadeth
    In the west with colors gay,
And we rest at last from labors
    Of the long and weary day.

Sweet is sunset, to my spirit,
    With its calm and mellow hour,
And its rich and ancient splendor
    O'er my soul has magic power.

For the sunbeams in my cottage,
    With their welcome glow of gold,
Are the same that shed their splendor
    There in happy days of old.

That is why I love the sunset's
    Mellow beauty on the floor,
For it wakes so many memories
    Of the halcyon days of yore.

THE WORLD'S WHEEL.

One success brings on another,
Each misfortune has its brother ;
That is the way the world's wheel goes,
'Tis a constant round of joys and woes.

MY EARLY DAYS.

My early days! my early days!
How fondly back on them I gaze.
How clear the stream flows where I strayed,
How fair the landscape where I played,
How fresh, how gushing was the joy
When I was but a thoughtless boy.

My early days! my early days!
No shadow dark upon them lays;
But when I catch their glimpses bright,
I feel a fresh and fond delight
That time and tide can ne'er destroy;
Oh! that I were once more a boy.

My early days! my early days!
When now I roam earth's weary ways
Full many a longing fills my heart,
To feel the joy they did impart;
But I have lost their bright decoy,
And nevermore will be a boy.

THE ROADSIDE FLOWER.

I saw a little flower one day,
That grew beside the dusty way
      With rich perfume ;
No velvet violet in the vale,
Or lakelet lily, sweet and pale,
      Surpassed its bloom.

Though other flowers in beauty stood
Upon the margin of the wood,
      And charmed my eye;
This one became my favorite flower,
It drank the sunshine, dew and shower,
      And smiling sky.

But walking on the lone roadside
One day, I saw my flower had died,
      Each leaf had flown ;
And on the spot where once it grew,
No bud or blossom met my view
      That I had known.

But when returned the smile of spring,
And merry birds sang on the wing,
      For flowers to rise,
And came the showers of fresh, warm rain,
My flower awoke and smiled again
      Unto the skies.

Sweet flower, what thou hast taught to me
Of dear ones, who no more I see,
      Dismisses pain ;
I learn from thee, though they are dead,
Though rain and snow falls o'er their head
      They 'll come again.

THE CAT.

A FABLE.

There lived a cat, a poor, lean thing,
With little art or cunning,
It caught no sparrow off the wing,
Nor oft excelled in running;
The housewife set it oft to route,
And often would have drowned it,
The children, wallowing it about,
More often kicked than crowned it.

But once there happened in the house,
A wife of keen discernment.
She saw him slyly track a mouse
With cunning and concernment,
And prophesied, as women can
Upon full many a matter,
That he would some day outwit man
And be a favorite ratter.

And true enough, the tale was told,
Nor was her genius cheated;
The cat, though ignorant of gold,
Is like a monarch treated.
He eats rich food on china ware,
Lays on the sofa lazy,
Is called a hero, every hair,
And bears the name of " Daisy."

BEAUTY.

Beauty! thou proud, yet crownless queen;
    Thou conqueror of the conqueror's soul!
Has any slave thy features seen
    And not succumbed to thy control?
If so, he has a wondrous power,
    Or is unblessed with ideal eyes;
He sees no splendor in the flower,
    Nor pleasure in the summer skies.

Although thy face, so proud and cold,
    Betrays a heart by warmth forsook,
It seems more natural than bold
    To take the luxury of a look;
For neath the splendor of thine eyes
    The loftiest feel it sweet to sway;
And though a serpent in disguise,
    Who can thy sweet voice disobey?

Although 'tis true earth's charms and joys
    Are flowers o'er a deep abyss,
And all who follow their decoys
    Must learn the treachery of their bliss;
That downfall haunts Ambition's rage;
    That pleasure is allied to pain;
A fool is happier than a sage;
    So reign! sweet tyrant, Beauty, reign!

WYOMING'S VALE.

Oh! dark was the day the Mohawk came
　　To fair Wyoming's vale,
And the breathing of his dreadful name
　　Made the pioneers turn pale ;
There were only a few to strike the blow,
　　But their hearts did valiant keep ;
And they sallied forth to meet the foe,
　　In the forest dark and deep.

On, on they went, o'er hills and dells,
　　Far from their native vale ;
When sudden, the forest rang with yells
　　That made the bravest quail ;
The rifle's knell and the hatchet's thud
　　Rose high in the revel dire,
Till those fair fields were red with blood,
　　And the wild beast left his lair.

They battled long, they battled well,
　　Till the ground with heaps was piled ;
But the tide, that band could never quell,
　　Rushed on like a tempest wild,
And fiercer grew the warwhoop's tone,
　　And the hatchet swifter sped ;
The red sun sank on his dazzling throne,
　　And they turned and wildly fled.

Then fell the sire with locks of snow,
　　The mother and her child ;
The maiden in her youthful glow
　　A captive was beguiled ;

And far on the night, a sheet of flame
　　Told earth an awful tale.
Oh! dark was the day the Mohawk came
　　To fair Wyoming's vale.

MAKE YOUR MARK.

Make your mark! keep toiling on;
　　With the anvil, sword or pen:
Work until the day has gone,
　　Like the ancient iron men.
Labor, more than gifts divine,
　　Wafts us on the wings of fame—
Saves us from oblivion dark,
　　And gives us an immortal name.
　　　　Make your mark!

Great men labored day and night,
　　That is how they climbed so high;
Inch by inch, they scaled the height,
　　Till their glory reached the sky.
Garner in the gems of lore,
　　Brighten talent, spark by spark,
Scale the mountain more and more,
　　　　Make your mark!

We received the light of life,
      And this reason's radiant fire
To promote a nation's thrife,
      And to raise each other higher;
Climb the height where glory shines,
      Shun oblivion's gulf so dark;
He's no hero who declines.
                  Make your mark !

Even the delver of the soil,
      Or the crier of the town,
May, by unremitting toil,
      Fill the world with his renown.
Let us then, toil day and night,
      Though at first the path be dark;
Strive to gain the glorious height.
                  Make your mark !

A CONSOLATION.

She was a tender flower of May,
      Whose promise brightened day by day;
But death came with his cruel knife
      And cut the tender cords of life.

Ah ! it is sad, but do not weep;
      Sweet and celestial is her sleep,
For e'er the soul had passed away
      The angels oped the gates of day.

THE LIGHT OF OTHER DAYS IS GONE.

The light of other days is gone,
    And silence dwells in rooms and halls.
A voice we used to dote upon
    Will sound no more within our walls;
A hand that soothed is laid to rest;
    A face that smiled has ceased to cheer;
A babe that pressed his mother's breast
    Will find she is no longer here.

About the house we come and go,
    The blinds are closed and all is still;
And in the rain or drifting snow
    We think of yonder lonely hill.
At eve the lamps we trim and light
    To kill the gloom with ruddy glare;
But one who made the household bright,
    Adorns no more the old arm chair.

Put out the fire and lock the door,
    Desert the old home in its gloom.
Since one we loved is here no more
    A sadness dwells in every room.
Take one that can a solace give,
    Or to some distant dwelling stray;
You cannot in the old home live,
    For mother dear, has passed away.

SWEET SLEEPS THE MOON UPON THE BAY.

Sweet sleeps the moon upon the bay,
    Where calm and still the waters lie;
With silver caps the ripples play
    Beneath the blue and tranquil sky.

The ships far out like phantoms stand
    And cast their shadows dark below.
No sound intrudes, as by command
    The gentlest zephyrs cease to blow.

Save to his lassie far away,
    The boatman plays his sweet guitar;
Or some gay sailor sings his lay
    And mounts toward the evening star.

How beautiful and how serene!
    Come, artist, paint a scene like this,
Inspired by that unrivalled queen
    That walks before the gates of bliss.

A RARE OLD BOOK.

Give me a book, a rare old book,
    And let the world roll on;
I shall not envy the miser's gold,
    Or care for the look of scorn;
I shall not covet the treasures bright,
    Or the rare gems 'neath the sea;
You may revel to your heart's delight,
    But a rare old book for me.

You may dance and sing with a happy heart,
    And laugh with women and wine;
You may struggle for fame in palace or cot,
    And walk in the paths that shine;
You may join in the chase for fortune fair,
    Whatever your lot may be;
Pray take your choice, for joy is rare,
    But leave an old book for me.

You may garnish halls with beauty bright,
    Throughout the busy day;
You may spread your board with luxuries light,
    And let the piano play;
You may gather the merry maidens in
    That fill the heart with glee,
But leave apart from the jolly din
    A rare old book for me.

THE HUDSON RIVER.

Grand was the scene a summer morn
    Adown the Hudson river;
The sun, who spilled his golden horn,
    Made waves with splendor quiver;
The hills each side majestic rose,
    Like lords who scorned promotion;
While, with a calm, sublime repose,
    The tide swept to the ocean.

I thought of the days, the storied days,
    When Hudson first sailed over,
And here he met the wondering gaze
    Of many a forest rover,
Who, (says a beautiful legend
    That claimed its source a fountain),
In tireless search their way did wend
    O'er valley brook and mountain.

For the Indians say this river then
    Was queen of Neptune's daughters;
Ah! then stood out, unmarred by men,
    The beauty of its waters.
Here Natuue must have sought display
    By all her grandeur massing,
If at this late prosaic day
    Her charms are so surpassing.

THE ROSES.

O royal rose, so full and bright!
    That blushes in the garden fair,
Bathed in the sunshine's warmest light,
    And filled with perfume, rich and rare;
Thou art the queen, the floral queen,
    Of all beneath the warm blue sky;
And through the summer hours serene,
    Thou charm'st the beauty-seeking eye.

Daughter of June! type of the fair,
    And token of affection's chain!
Some sister beauty thee shall wear.
    Who but a summer day shall reign?
In halls of splendor thou shalt shine,
    Amid the merry, bright and gay,
Or sadly in the funeral shrine
    Thy charms shall fade and pass away.

Alas! that beauty such as thine
    Must perish in a summer's day;
And all the fairest flowers that shine
    Are born to blush and pass away.
If all the beauties here must die,
    That shine like thee, with royal pride,
What gems of splendor, must there lie
    In that fair realm beyond the skies.

FAME.

Proud princess Fame! so frail and cold,
    The tyrant idol of the great!
What is thy beauty to behold?
    To whom art thou the happy mate,
That men should pay so dear a price;
    And kings should at thy footstool bow,
And wade through battle, toil and strife
    To wear thy laurels on their brow ?

Although for thee some spirits feel
    A passion useless to resist,
Thy sunniest smile is cold as steel,
    Thy form is like a fleeting mist
That leads the charmed adventurer on
    Through many a dark and thorny way,
Where dauntless starers stand around
    To shut him from the light of day.

Yet not in vain! not all in vain!
    Are sentiments thou dost inspire;
The loyal heart oft joins thy train,
    And climbs the mountain higher and higher;
And though the bounty of thy smile
    Is fraught with burdens to the soul,
He takes grim pleasure in the tax,
    And helps the tide of progress roll.

THE GOSSIPS.

I can forbear
With bores that wear,—
    With the din of the noisy Lossips,
I can forgive the rustic stare,
    But I do detest the gossips.

Who hear, say, bring
And know each thing
    But necessary labors,
Who leave the babe to squall and sing,
    And run to see the neighbors;

Who raise a tale
On Mrs. Gale,
    And herald it and sell it;
Then with big eyes, and faces pale,
    Tell others not to tell it;

Who know Miss B,
Her pedigree,
    Her sisters and her brothers;
Who tattle all they hear or see
    About themselves and others;

Who watch and wait
To hear Miss Gate
    Receive her lover, Harry,
And wonder why he staid so late,
    And when they are to marry.

Oh! I can forbear
With bores that wear,
    With the din of the noisy Lossips,
I oft forgive the rustic stare,
    But I do detest the gossips.

THAT BEAUTEOUS DREAM.

That beauteous dream will come no more,
　　That entertained my early days,
And oft beguiled my fancy bright
　　To roam in earth's exalted ways.
Those images of lofty joy
　　That smiled in Flattery's gilded halls,
Fate's cruel hand would fain destroy,
　　But Time his power yet enthralls.

Once glowing hope and youthful fire
　　Made mountains seem inferior things;
I deemed it not a wild desire
　　To rise to eminence with wings;
But struggles vain for petty spoil,
　　The blight of hopes, the tide of need,
Tells me it is one thing to toil
　　And quite another to succeed.

But then, why should I lose the way,
　　And wander in the desert dark,
Where shrines of worth will soon decay,
　　And none have ever made their mark?
'Tis a glorious deed, to nobly plan
　　To battle, though we lose the fight,
And he who strives to be a man,
　　Becomes a hero in God's sight.

BEN BUTLER'S WOOING.

Ben Butler is a whole-souled man,
    With large, ingenious brain;
To help his fellows all he can
    Seems his object more than gain.
He has his failings, all men know,
    For none are pure as blueing;
But I have got no stone to throw —
    I'll tell you of his wooing.

He had a damsel fair to see,
    Whom he with ardor courted,
He walked her on the lonely lea,
    And oft to church escorted;
But there were rival beaux to rout,
    Accomplished, deft and handsome;
He found it hard to court them out,
    And his heart refused all ransom.

But near his cherished lady's house
    A little streamlet wandered,
And being cunning as a mouse,
    He often by it pondered;
This they must cross to gain her side —
    Their fondness is unceasing.
Ah! I will make a slippery slide,
    I'll give this log a greasing.

So coming in his brand new blend,
　　With hearty inward laughter,
He greased the log from end to end,
　　His careful footsteps after;
Then with a satisfactory smile
　　Upon his cunning features,
He hastened to alone beguile
　　The prettiest of creatures.

He talked a while of Cupid rash,
　　Of Samson and Darius;
When suddenly there came a splash
　　And phrases all but pious,
A scramble to the other brink,
　　A step and all was over;
But none went home, I dare to think,
　　With tempers sweet as clover.

But ah! alas, for well won joys
　　So soon to be defeated,
For when he left her sweet decoys
　　And toward his home retreated,
Wrapt in the ecstasy of bliss,
　　With head in glory tossing,
His soul burned with that last sweet kiss—
　　And knew no slippery crossing.

He bravely stepped upon the log,
　　A deep, cold stream was running,
What was that splash? Was it a frog?
　　Or urchins rashly funning?

Was it a man? Was it a cat
    That struggled with such vigor?
It looked more like a drownéd rat,
    But was a great deal bigger.

He climbed the stairs with little thought
    About the feminine gender,
But though their charms he quite forgot,
    He never did surrender;
So off he started once again,
    To be the bridal broachman,
But oh! how disappointments pain,
    She eloped with a favorite coachman!

———

THE SECRET WELL.

Far down in the heart,
Like the deep, deep sea,
The soul has a secret well
Where images reflected, shine,
That poets alone can tell.

NAPOLEON'S GRAVE.

Far on a bleak and barren shore,
    They sadly laid him down;
The hero monarchs knelt before
    The winner of a crown,
And there the seabird's mournful cry
    Rang through the caverns dim;
And those majestic cliffs on high
    Were all that seemed like him.

There did the willow sadly weep
    With melancholy tone,
As if aware that he in sleep
    Once knew a dazzling throne;
There did the billows charge and roar
    And rush in headlong flight,
As if they knew the power he bore
    And sought to show his might.

There does the pensive traveller tread
    With soft, instinctive awe;
There does the proudest bend his head,
    For reverance there is law;
There scenes of glory on him steal;
    He sees the grand review;
And hears the last faint thunder peal
    That died at Waterloo.

Sleep, loftiest man in days of yore!
   Proud type of Rome and Greece !
That long and mighty strife is o'er ;
   And Europe rests in peace;
But what is power and proud parade,
   With crowns and splendor grand ;
For here the mightiest king was laid,
   Far from his native land.

THE DAYS OF CHIVALRY.

O for the days,
   The good old days,
The days of chivalry,
   When gallant knights
Fought many fights
   For ladies fair to see;
When warriors true
   Came oft to woo,
And sang so merrily.
   O for the days,
The good old days,
   The days of chivalry !

O for the days,
   The good old days,
When hearts were free from fear;
   When o'er the land,
With sword in hand,
   Roamed many a cavalier,

Who bold did ride
    To win his bride,
In distant halls of glee.
    O for the days,
The good old days,
    The days of chivalry!

O for the days,
    The good old days,
The days of chivalry,
    When gallant deeds
And noble steeds
    Were more than royalty;
When love controlled
    The lust for gold,
And hearts were warm and free,
    O for the days,
The good old days,
    The days of chivalry.

LIFE.

Life, surely, is a game of chance,
Where many demons seem to dance,
But even so, I'll venture brave,
For win or lose, there frowns the grave.

TOUSSAINT'S SOLILOQUY.

And am I thus to die, —
In this dark dungeon where afflictions dwell ?
Why was I banished so ?
So banished from my home, my native land !
Oh ! what sweet words unto a patriot's soul ;
To him, they mean his mother and his love, —
His father's glory and his children's smile, —
His precious freedom, dearer than his life ;
And all his joys, ·his sorrows, hopes and fears.
Alas ! why was I thus unjustly wronged ?
It was to satisfy a freeborn slave !
A slave to vile Ambition's curséd fire !
Because, indignant at the monster wrong,
I rose and rivalled his most brilliant deeds !
For those achievements do I suffer now ;
But ah ! how sweet to die a hero's death ; —
To die that fellow mortals may be free.
Not always on the field of blood and fire
Are noblest sacrifices made for man.
Like hidden treasures in the ocean's depths,
Some forms have sunk to seal their dearest wish ;
Some mother perished for her only child —
Some youth or maiden for a dear one's weal ;
Then, oh ! how sweet to die a patriot's death.
These rugged stones become a bed of flowers ; —
This galling chain—has turned to burnished gold.
Behold ! the gates of light ! Beat back the dark.
Is this the same old dungeon as of yore ?
I thought I was a captive, but 'tis false ; —
My links they tremble, and my heart grows cold ;

But all my soul is filled with wondrous joy !
Ah ! I am dying ! Yes, my race is run ;
But he shall live to meet a bitter fate, —
A fate far worse than death in misery !

———

MAN.

Oh ! what is man ?   A mockery of might,
A victim to each petty whim and snare.
He seeks in vain for peace and happiness;
And struggles on for what he ne'er attains.
A lord of all creation, yet its slave ;
He struts about in fickle dignity.
How grand is he when blessed with wealth and power ;
How mean and humble when in penury !
'Tis true that he is dangerous when equipped,
But when unarmed how abject is his state ;
He dare not face the smallest beast enraged,
And flees in terror at the hornet's wrath.
How marvelous a work could be conceived ;
With all the contradictions found in man !

THE ASSASSIN'S DREAM.

Away, Sir Reginald! get thee away!
But give my spirit one small moment's peace,
And all I gained that night, by that foul deed,
I will bequeath to thy inheritors.
Ha! that dark night within that lonely room,
How flashed my dagger as I crept anear
Until it found his unsuspecting heart.
Since then what raging fire has filled my soul!
And in the calmest night born for repose, —
I see a thousand demons dancing 'round;
Then, if I close my eyes I see them still.
Oh! could I but undo that awful deed;
For in the day sometimes they torment so —
I fear that some read murder in my eyes.
Last night I dreamed I was a boy once more;
And as I roamed the fields with careless joy,
The tempter rose from earth as unto Eve,
Full many golden apples offered her ;
And not until the sunshine left his head
Did I perceive his awful hideousness.
I fled away across the hills with speed ;
But soon he seized me with his many arms;
And though I struggled in a maniac's zeal
He bound me tight and bore me to his den.
Then I awoke, but oh! how beat my heart ;
Cold perspiration stood upon my brow;
And all my frame shook like an aspen leaf.
I started to cry out — my tongue was dumb —
Oh! had I but that dagger by my side,
There would its blade have found a final sheath.
This awful plight I can no longer stand, —
I must confess or throw my life away.

JOAN OF ARC'S DEFIANCE.

Think not I fear the flames;
Such dooms as this can never harm the soul.
Even now I hear the voices call again
And tell me well my mission is fulfilled.

Even now do I behold sweet Margaret's eyes,
With Michael strong and Catharine so mild;
Soon shall I join them where their glory shines; —
And look triumphant on this smouldering pile.

Cast on the fagots, for the more they blaze
The greater shall my crown of glory be;
And were it not for Satanic conceit
I fain would thrust my arm within the blaze; —
But deeds like that ill suit a martyr's fame; —
It is for me to suffer and be true.

O France! O Domehery — beloved, sweet vale!
I would that I might die a thousand deaths
In sacrificing for my fatherland.
Think not a woman's heart will always fail;
For in the frail bodies oft the staunchest beat.

And these mad flames that soon shall wreath my form
Shall show your bitter spite but harm me not.
Yes, their consuming power will be your curse; —
But in their glare I shall be glorified.

CLEOPATRA.

Art thou a Cleopatra come to life,
With every little type of beauty blessed ?
I scorn to be a slave to cruel charms,
Or lose my judgment from a favoring glance;
But now I feel my merits sink to nought,
And take a slavish spell hard to explain.
How sweet to dwell neath those voluptuous eyes !
I must confess, though rather stern at heart,
I feel my senses swaying as from wine,
And leaving plots to feast 'mid beauty's dream.
Oh! mighty Cæsar may have done the same,
With all his love of war and greed of power.
Such charms intoxicate the sternest will,
And he is bold indeed as any brave
Who dares to be a rival for thy hand.
No wonder Anthony forgot his sword
To revel in his love's exquisite arms,
If Cleopatra was as fair as thee !
For even now some would forsake a throne,
To be a petty servant at thy feet,
In hopes of catching glances from thine eyes.

TACT.

'Tis quite an art your tongue to still
    When there's no recompense,
To treat the wounded heart with skill
    And blame without offense.

JESSIE'S GRAVE.

Soft sighs the trees,
Sweet blows the breeze
    Where gentle Jessie lies;
Long hangs the hour,
Sad nods the flower
    Beneath the summer skies.

I listen long
To the blithe bird's song,
    Amid the summer's dream;
And my thoughts repose,
As my eyelids close,
    Like yonder placid stream.

Rest, sainted child,
Mid the summer mild,
    So beautiful, like thee.
But I heave a sigh
That you should die,
    Fair queen of chivalry.

LORD BYRON TO THE GREEKS.

Strong men of Greece, sons of heroic blood
Spilled at Thermopylæ and Marathon!
I call ye to the battle once again
To resurrect the glories of her urn.
Let not the vile Ottoman trample on
And sully in the dust thy spotless flag,
Whose fame was won on many a field of blood!
Long has it been since war thy shores awoke,
And called thee on to spoils and victory;
But now the hour of triumph has arrived,
And Turkey's dastard blades shall win no more.
Awake! ye gods of history, awake!
Where is that blood that Leonidas led?
Where is that blood that, when the Romans came,
Drove them in desperation from the field?
Where is that fire Demosthenes inspired?
And all the glories of the tongue and pen?
Ah! they have slept too long, brave men of Greece.
Awake! and let old Athens shine once more!

VALOR.

Sing not of splendid daring in the field,
    And of renowned adventurers alone;
For they but battle on to gather spoil;
    And gain the pomp and glory of a throne.
Oft have I seen far braver deeds performed
    Without the trumps and blazonry of fame;
And of them, one is how a valiant girl
    Watched by my mother's and my sister's side.

BARNEY GLYNN'S COURTSHIP.

Cold was the night when Barney Glynn
Decided to call on his girl, Mary Flynn.

For he had loved her long and well,
But knew not how that love to tell.

So, putting many a fear to rout,
He now determined to let it out.

He was a son of Erin's Isle,
With a paratoed walk and a blarney smile.

She was a broad and buxom dame,
With looks and manners much the same.

He had blacked his boots and combed his hair,
And he said to himself, " We 'll make a foine pair."

But some would have laughed, I suppose, like galoots,
As he hummed, and smoked, with his pants in his boots.

The light was lit with a bright galore,
So he boldly knocked at the kitchen door.

She came to the door with her face all red, —
" The weathor is foine," was all he said.

She was all embarrassed, though wrapt in bliss,
So all she could manage to say was " Yis."

He took a seat in a handy chair,
And looked around with a vacant stare.

She took a seat not far away,
But turned all colors — red, blue and gray.

They gave not a sign, they spoke not a word ;
The rats in the ceiling was all they heard.

He peeked at her and she peeked at him,
And so they sat, till the light grew dim.

Then he struggled hard to conquer dismay,
But " The weathor is foine," was all he could say,

And she seemed to be in equal distress,
For all she could think of to answer was, " Yis. "

In his brand new boots, he started to go;
When he tripped on the stove leg, hurting his toe.

The kettle was full and all in a roar,
But Barney and the stove both sprawled on the floor.

He struggled to rise from the floor, scarcely able,
When his back struck a leaf and tipped over the table.

The landlady, thinking the " divil " to pay,
Rushed down in the kitchen in wild dismay.

All excited, bewildered, and just out of bed,
She thought Barney a burglar, and beat on his head.

He heard in the distance, the watch-dog draw near,
So he dashed through the window, and fled like a steer ;

But the canine already was hot in the chase,
And they went down the road in a beautiful race.

He tried to look back in a lightning glance,—
The savage grabbed hold of his best Sunday pants.

They fumbled and fumed and struggled away ;
He climbed up a tree and staid till next day;

Then he scrambled down, with a wild, pallid face,
And trudged sadly home, 'neath a load of disgrace.

And he went to the farm, to his hard daily work,
Though he looked like a clothes-line, and felt like a shirk.

Poor Barney, all beaten, bewildered and sore,
Determined to venture a-courting no more ;

But for all his great hardships, trials and pain,
He determined, one evening, to see her again.

And after remaining another long hour,
He spoke, from an effort of wonderful power.

Yes, he finally managed to speak to his miss,
And even the daring to give her a kiss.

And now, hero Barney throws lots in the shade, —
He has bought a small farm, and won a " foine " maid.

WOMEN AND WINE.

What founts of eloquence divine
Are wasted over women and wine; —
How fickle both are like the breeze
And set their victims ill at ease,
Yet still we like them more and more
Because they cheer our hearts so poor.
'Tis certain when their powers beguile
We feel much braver for a while,
And when we meet them rich and bright
They fill us with a rare delight, —
But woe to him who is so blind
To favor long the giddy kind.

————

SUNSET IN AUTUMN.

See where the gorgeous splendor brims the hills,
And fills the skies with many tinted hues !
What throne of radiance e'er surpassed that scene ?
What Oriental splendor mingles there !
The artist strives to catch the rich array,
But how his deftest brush and genius bright
Has failed to give the touch so marvellous.

ADDRESS TO THE OCEAN.

Ye rippling waters, rolling on unchecked,
Like man's conception of eternity,
How dreadful, how sublime, how great thou art!
Encircling all the world within thy arms;
The stately ships, that on thy bosom ride,
Are tempest tossed, to please thy mighty will;
Within thy depths they sink, and do no harm;
Just like the monsters nursed upon thy breast,
They rush with fearful power, yet are thy toys.
What shores feel not thy touch? Where is thy end?
Who can conceive thy depths, thy vast domain?
The forest, without limit, can be hewn;
But who can check or lessen thy resource?
The sun, with all his heat and wondrous power,
Drinks from thy flood, but can obscure thee not.
Thou rollest ever on in endless space;
Now calm and tranquil as a glassy lake,—
Now in thine anger dashing mountains high.
Though man, with all his skill and science great,
Is often at thy mercy prone to fall,
He, who with but a word, has called thee forth,
Can with a word create or still thy wave.

INDEX.